Beginning
CHARTS, GR...
and DIAGRAMS

Skill Building Activities for the Primary Child

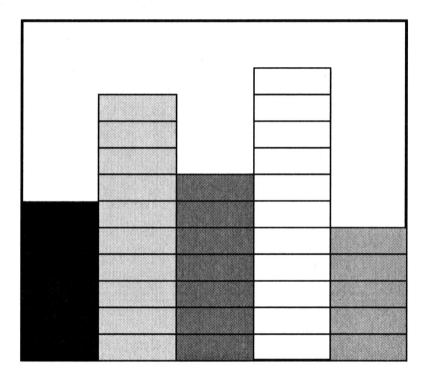

Written by John and Patty Carratello
Illustrated by Paula Spence and Keith Vasconcelles

Teacher Created Materials, Inc.
6421 Industry Way
Westminster, CA 92683
www.teachercreated.com
©1990 Teacher Created Materials, Inc.
Reprinted, 2002
Made in U.S.A.
ISBM-1-55734-168-0

Table of Contents

Introduction

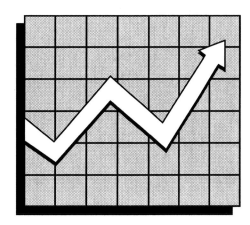

Beginning Charts, Graphs, and Diagrams

One of a child's earliest opportunities to communicate with others is through pictures. He learns the ideas of others when he looks at picture and talks about what he sees. She lets others know what she is thinking when she draws a picture and tells an interested person about what she has drawn.

Charts, graphs, and diagrams *are pictures. They are visual ways to communicate information about all kinds of things—from the types of pets owned by students in your class, or the population of various countries in the world, to the parts of a bicycle. From charts, graphs, and diagrams, a child can learn a wealth of information about the world in which he or she lives.*

Beginning Charts, Graphs, and Diagrams *contains activities geared to primary children who are learning basic skills and about these visual tools. Each tool is explained and examined thoroughly, and followed by interesting reinforcement activities.*

We know that through the successful completion of the activities in this book, your children will have the basic skills it takes to become visually literate readers and makers of charts, graphs, and diagrams.

What Are Charts, Graphs, and Diagrams?

Charts, graphs, and **diagrams** are visual tools. They give us a way to see information easily. It is sometimes easier to see information in a chart, graph, or diagram than to *hear* it or *read* it.

Read these results of a survey taken in a second grade class of 30 students. They were asked the month of their birth.

Three were born in January, five in February, and none in March. April had four student birthdays, and May had seven. There were two birthdays in both June and July, and three in August. September had two, and both October and November had one. There were no class birthdays in December.

Now, look at the same information presented in a chart, graph, and diagram. Is it easier for you to understand when you can see it?

Chart of Class Birthdays

Month	Number of Birthdays
January	3
February	5
March	0
April	4
May	7
June	2
July	2
August	3
September	2
October	1
November	1
December	0

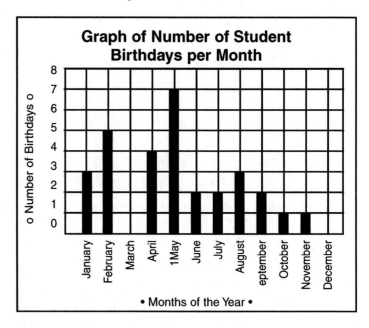

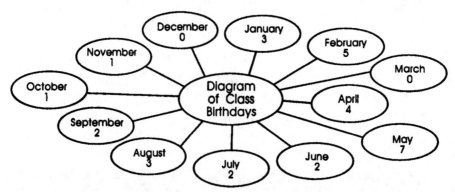

Read the Picture!

We can read words and understand what someone wants us to know. We can also read pictures!

Read these pictures and answer the questions.

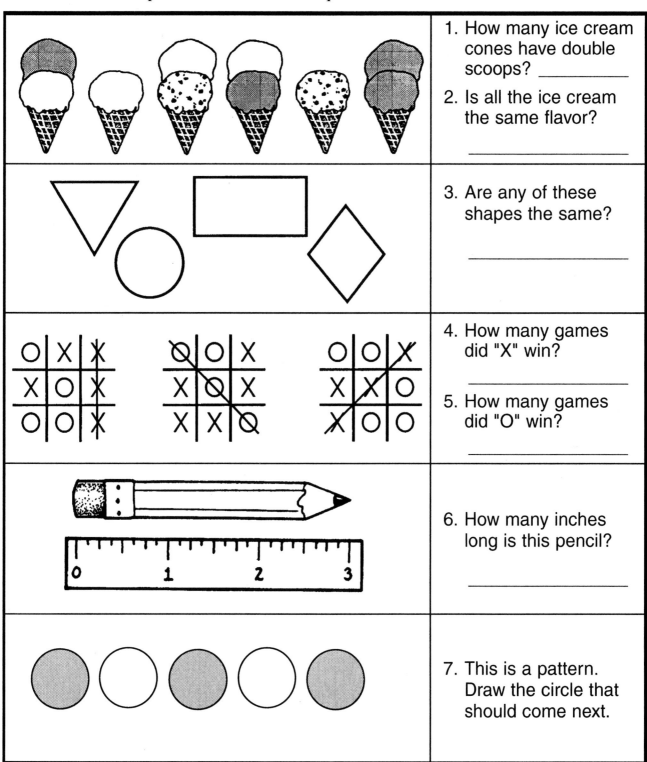

1. How many ice cream cones have double scoops? _____

2. Is all the ice cream the same flavor?

_____

3. Are any of these shapes the same?

_____

4. How many games did "X" win?

_____

5. How many games did "O" win?

_____

6. How many inches long is this pencil?

_____

7. This is a pattern. Draw the circle that should come next.

Can you read pictures?

Draw the Picture!

Show that you understand the words on this page by drawing the pictures to explain them.

	One of the balloons has popped. It was not the same color as the others.
	The rectangle is larger than the square.
	One of the candles has been blown out.
	Six different colors are marked on the wall.
	One of the balls is different.

By the Number

A very easy type of chart to use is a number and color chart. Just read across the chart to find out what color to use for each number you see in the picture.

Color this picture by using the numbers and colors in the chart.

Color by the Number	
number	color to use
1	green
2	blue
3	gray
4	brown

What Color, Please?

Make your own color chart for this picture. Then color the picture in the colors you chose for the chart.

number	color to use
1	
2	
3	
4	
5	
6	
7	

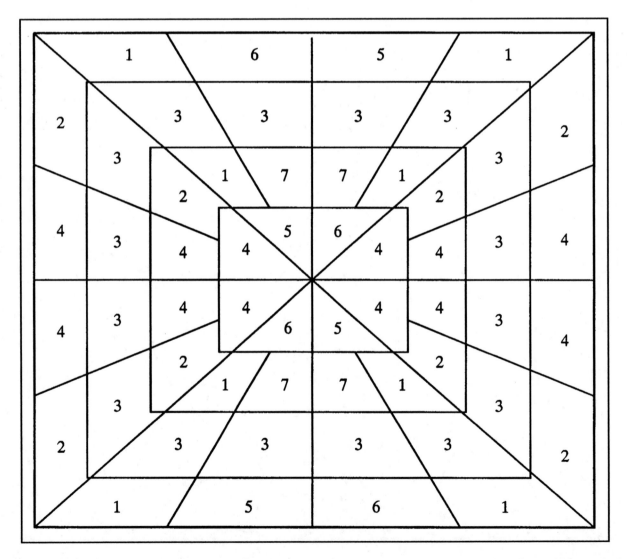

How Much Is It Worth?

Read this money chart. Then answer the questions.

Pennies, Nickels, and Dimes

$$1¢ + 1¢ + 1¢ + 1¢ + 1¢ = 5¢$$

$$5¢ + 5¢ = 10¢$$

$$1¢ + 1¢ + 1¢ + 1¢ + 1¢$$
$$1¢ + 1¢ + 1¢ + 1¢ + 1¢ = 10¢$$

1. A penny is worth _____ .

2. A nickel is worth _____ .

3. A dime is worth _____ .

4. ____ pennies equal ____ nickel.

5. ____ nickels equal _____ dime.

6. _____ pennies equal _____ dime.

7. 5 pennies equal _____ .

8. 2 nickels equal _____ .

9. 10 pennies equal _____ .

10. 1 dime, 1 nickel, and 1 penny
    equal _____ .

Tally Charts

We can keep a record of how many things we count on a piece of paper. An easy way to do this is to make a **tally chart.**

For every thing you count, you make a mark like this: |

To make it easier and faster to read, every fifth mark is crossed over the four marks that come before it like this: |||||

How many marks are there? _____

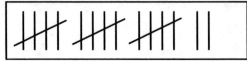

How many marks are there? _____

It is easier to count by fives than it is to count by ones on a tally chart.

Read these tally charts. Write how many marks each tally has.

||||| | = ___ ||||| ||||| ||||| | = ___ ||||| |||| = ___

||||| ||||| ||||| ||||| | = ___ ||||| ||||| = ___ |||| = ___

Make tally charts for the numbers in the boxes below.

= 5	= 10
=7	= 13
= 9	= 17

Favorite Subject

The students in Mr. Lockwood's class took a class vote to find out what subject was liked most by class members. MR. Lockwood kept a record of the votes for each subject on a tally chart.

Read the chart. Then answer the questions.

Our Favorite Subjects	
Subject	**Tally of Votes**
mathematics	|||
art	||||
history		
science	|||||
music	||
reading	|||||	
writing	|||
physical education	|||||
health		

1. What subject is liked the most? _____

   How many people like it the most? _____

2. What subjects tied for second place?

   _____ and _____

3. Did any subjects tie with writing? _____

4. Was mathematics more liked than history? _____

5. Did these students like art more than music? _____

Our Favorite Subject Tally Chart

Take a class vote to find out what the favorite subjects are in your class. Ask your teacher to count the votes for each subject and tell you the numbers. Keep a record of the votes on this tally sheet. Then answer the questions at the bottom of the page.

Our Favorite Subjects	
Subject	**Tally of Votes**
mathematics	
art	
history	
science	
music	
reading	
writing	
physical education	
health	

1. What subject is liked the most? _____

   How many people like it? _____

2. Is math or science liked more? _____

3. Is writing or reading liked more? _____

4. Were there any subjects without a vote? _____

5. What is your favorite subject? _____

Movie Time!

Mr. Harrison asked his second grade students what their favorite movies were. They came up with a list of ten they really liked. Mr. Harrison asked the children to vote for their favorite ones by raising their hands. This is what the hand count looked like. Mr. Harrison voted, too!

Write the results of this class vote on the chart.

Favorite Movies of Mr. Harrison's Class			
Movie Title	votes	**Movie Title**	votes
Bambi		E.T.	
Lady and the Tramp		Oliver and Company	
Heroes in a Halfshell		The Karate Kid	
Superman		Transformers	
The Land Before Time		Cinderella	

1. What is the most popular movie in Mr. Harrison's class? _____
   How many votes? _____

2. What movie do they like second best? _____

3. What movies tied for third place? _____

4. What movie do you think Mr. Harrison voted for? _____

5. What movie do you like most from this list? _____

*Conduct A Movie Vote In **Your** Class!*

What's Your Pet?

Ask the students in your class what kind of pets they have at home. Some students may have more than one pet and other students may have no pets at all.

Keep a tally of what you find out. Then answer the questions below the chart.

Pets Owned By People In My Class	
turtles	horses
dogs	cats
mice	fish
birds	hamsters
snakes	frogs
chicken	lizards
gerbils	rabbits
(other)	(other)
(other)	(other)

1. What kind of pet is owned more than others? _____

2. Are there more cat owners or dog owners? _____

3. Are there more bird owners or fish owners? _____

4. What is the most unusual pet in the class? _____

5. What pets to you own? _____

Table of Contents

A *table of contents* in the front of a book or magazine is a type of chart. The table tells you very quickly what is inside the book or magazine and where to find it.

> Read this table of contents. Then answer the questions.

The Book of Unusual Pets

by Ima Lizard

---

1. Does this book give reasons why people might like unusual pets? _____
   _____On what page? _____

2. On what pages can we start to find out about:
   gerbils? _____ ducks? _____ snakes? _____

3. What animal is talked about in:
   Chapter 3? _____ Chapter 7? _____

4. In what chapter would you look to find out more about monkeys? On what page?

   _____

5. Can this book help you find an unusual pet? _____
   On what page? _____

* Which chapter would we look in to find out about the pet in this book that you are
   most interested in? _____

You Make One!

Make a table of contents to fit this book description.

* The name of the book is **_Dinosaurs._**

* The author of the book is Ty Rex.

* There are five chapters in the book.

* Every chapter is about a different dinosaur.

* The chapters are in alphabetical order, by the name of the dinosaur.

* Each chapter is five pages long.

* The names of the dinosaurs in the book are: Pteranodon, Triceratops, Stegosaurus, Tyrannosaurus, and Apatosaurus.

_____

by

_____

Chapter 1: _____ page 3

Chapter 2: _____ page 8

Chapter 3: _____ page 13

Chapter 4: _____ page _____

Chapter 5: _____ page _____

What To Do After School

Billy has five different things he likes to do after school. He does each one of them on a certain day.

This is his activity schedule.

Monday: Piano lessons

Tuesday: Baseball practice

Wednesday: Baking cookies

Thursday: Bike riding with friends

Friday: Painting pictures

A *calendar* is a type of chart. Make a calendar for Billy. cut out these pictures of the activities Billy does. Attach them to the correct days on the calendar found on page 18. Use the activity schedule to help you.

painting

baseball

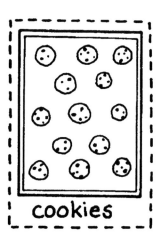

cookies

biking

Which of the things that Billy likes to do after school do you like to do also?

_____

_____

_____

_____

piano

Afterschool Activities

Attach the afterschool activities found on page 17 in the correct days on this calendar.

Afterschool Activities I Like To Do and When I'm Going To Do Them!	Monday
Tuesday	**Wednesday**
Thursday	**Friday**

Make your own afterschool activities calendar!

What Michelle Does

Michelle and her parents keep a chart of things Michelle has to do each week. When she does them without being told, her parents draw a happy face in the box below the thing she has done on the day she does it. This way, Michelle always knows what she has to do without her parents reminding her to do it. Michelle feels good about herself for being responsible. Her parents are very proud of her, too!

These are the things Michelle has done this week. Pretend you are one of her parents. Draw a happy face on the chart on page 20 to show what Michelle has done.

Sunday

- Walked the dogs
- Made her bed
- Fed the animals
- Practiced the piano

Monday

- Fed the animals
- Made her bed
- Emptied the wastebaskets
- Walked the dogs
- Did her homework

Tuesday

- Fed the animals
- Made her bed
- Did her homework
- Practiced the piano
- Walked the dogs

Wednesday

- Fed the animals
- Made her bed
- Did her homework
- Practiced the piano
- Did the dishes

Thursday

- Fed the animals
- Made her bed
- Emptied the wastebaskets
- Did her homework

Friday

- Fed the animals
- Made her bed
- Walked the dogs
- Practiced the piano

Saturday

- Fed the animals
- Practiced the piano
- Did the dishes
- Emptied the wastebaskets

Michelle's Chart

(Use the information on page 19 to complete this chart.)

My Chart of Jobs / Days	Feed the animals every day.	Empty the baskets 3 times a week.	Practice the piano 5 times a week.	Do your homework when it is assigned.	Make your bed daily.	Walk the dogs three times a week.	Do the dishes three times a week.
Sunday							
Monday							
Tuesday							
Wednesday							
Thursday							
Friday							
Saturday							
Did Michelle do what she needed to do this week?	Yes			Yes			

My Responsibilities

Work with your parents to create your own job chart. Have fun!

My Chart of Jobs *Jobs* Days								
Sunday								
Monday								
Tuesday								
Wednesday								
Thursday								
Friday								
Saturday								
Did you do what you needed to do this week?								

Notes for Special Times

Mrs. Lenai likes to mail a special calendar to the parents of the children who will soon be in her class. On the calendar, there are dates of activities that will happen during the school year. She also writes any other information a parent might need about these activities in the calendar boxes. Mrs. Lenai says that parents like to receive these calendars early because it helps them plan their year, too!

> Here are Mrs. Lenai's notes about what she wants to write on the calendar. She has started writing them on the calendar, but has left out some information. Use her notes to complete the calendar on page 23.

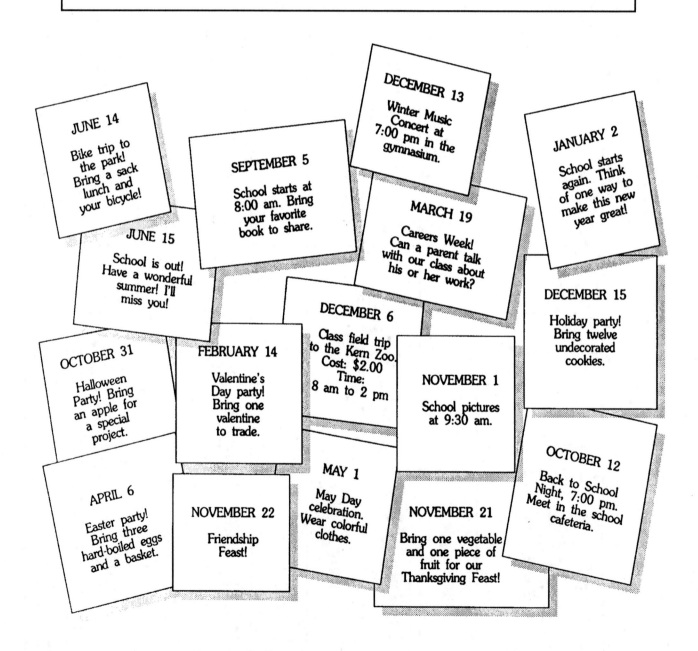

Parent Calendar

Use the teacher's notes on page 22 to help you fill in this calendar of school activities.

Special Times in Our School Year

September 5	**October 12**	**October 31**	**November 1**
School starts! _____ a.m. Bring your favorite _____ to share!	Back to School Night! _____ p.m. Meet in the school _____ .	_____ Party! Bring an _____ for a special project.	School _____ _____ a.m. 
November 21	**November 22**	**December 6**	**December 13**
Bring one _____ and one piece of _____ for our _____ Feast!	_____ Feast! 	Class Field Trip to the _____ Cost: _____ Time: _____	Winter _____ Concert at _____ p.m. in the _____ .
December 15	**January 2**	**February 14**	**March 19**
_____ Party! Bring _____ undecorated _____ .	School starts again! Think of one way to make this New Year _____ !	Valentine's Day Party! Bring one _____ to trade. 	_____ Week! Can a parent talk with our class about his or her _____ ?
April 6	**May 1**	**June 14**	**June 15**
Easter Party! Bring _____ hard-boiled _____ and a _____ .	_____ Celebration! Wear _____ clothes! 	_____ trip to the _____ ! Bring a sack _____ and your _____ !	School is _____ ! Have a wonderful _____ ! I'll miss you!

Distance Chart

A **distance chart** tells you how far it is between two places if you travel by road to get there.

Here is how to read a distance chart.

1. Find the name of a place on the left side of the chart. Mark the place with your left finger.

2. Find the name of a place you would like to know the distance to at the top of the chart. Mark the place with your right finger.

3. To find the distance between these two places, slide your left finger straight across and your right finger straight down until they meet. You have found the distance!

Read the distance chart. Then answer the questions next to the chart.

Teacher Note: Distance may be measured in miles or kilometers.

Distance Chart	the ocean	the mountains	the zoo	the park	my school
my house	105	30	10	3	1
the ocean		135	95	108	104
the mountains	135		40	28	31
the zoo	95	40		13	9
the park	108	28	13		4

What is the distance from…

1. the ocean to the park? _____

2. my house to the mountains? _____

3. the zoo to the park? _____

4. the ocean to the mountains? _____

5. the zoo to my school? _____

6. my house to the park? _____

7. the ocean to my school? _____

How Far?

Use the distance chart on this page to answer the questions.

1. What six cities are on the distance chart?

   _____ , _____ , _____ ,

   _____ , _____ , and _____

2. How far is it from:

   a) Montreal to Los Angeles? _____ b) Chicago to Boston? _____

   c) New York City to Seattle? _____ d) Chicago to Montreal? _____

   e) New York City to Boston? _____ f) Los Angeles to Seattle? _____

3. What city is farthest from : a) New York? _____

   b) Los Angeles? _____ c) Seattle? _____

4. What city is closest to: a) Boston? _____

   b) Los Angeles? _____ c) Chicago? _____

Six City Distance Chart (computed in miles)	Boston	Chicago	Los Angeles	Montreal	New York City
Chicago	963		2054	828	802
Los Angeles	2779	2054		2873	2786
Montreal	318	828	2873		378
New York City	206	802	2786	378	
Seattle	2976	2013	1131	2685	2815

Use the chart form on page 74 to do this same exercise using kilometers.

Science Project

When we do a project in science, we keep a record of what we do and what we find out.

An easy way to keep a record is to write the information on a *chart*.

Study this chart. Then answer the questions below.

Record of Plant Growth	
Week of Observation	*Centimeters of Growth*
week 1 (Monday)	0 centimeters
week 2 (Monday)	2 centimeters
week 3 (Monday)	4 centimeters
week 4 (Monday)	8 centimeters
week 5 (Monday)	12 centimeters
week 6 (Monday)	20 centimeters
week 7 (Monday)	22 centimeters
week 8 (Monday)	26 centimeters

1. In which week was there no growth of the plant? _____

2. How many centimeters did the plant grow between week 2 and week 3?

   _____.

   Between which two charted weeks did the plant grow most? _____
   There was something done differently between these two weeks. What was done
   differently? _____

4. At the end of the recorded experiment, how tall was the plant? _____

5. Do you think the plant continued to grow? _____

Chart Your Results!

Arlene decided to do a science experiment to find out whether people used more water when they took a bath or a shower. This is what she found out.

- Her father used 16 centimeters of water when he took a bath. The next day, he took a shower with the plug in the shower drain. After he left the bathroom, Arlene measured the shower water. It was 20 centimeters.

- Her older sister used 10 centimeters of water for a bath and 12 centimeters of water for a shower.

- Her mother used 24 centimeters of water for a bath and 10 centimeters of water for a shower.

Chart the results of her experiment.

Then answer the questions below.

Water Used for Baths and Showers		
Person	Bath Water	Shower Water
father		
sister		
mother		

1. What family member should take a shower to save water?

2. What family member used almost the same amount of water in both a bath and a shower?

3. Who used the most water for a shower?

*Try this at home. Maybe you can help **your** family save water!*

Flow Charts

A flow chart shows, step by step, how something happens in the order it happens.

1. A child holds a packet of flower seeds.

2. The child plants the seeds.

3. The child waters the plant that has begun to grow.

4. The child enjoys the beautiful flowers.

Look at the scrambled flow chart below. Number the way these steps really **should** happen.

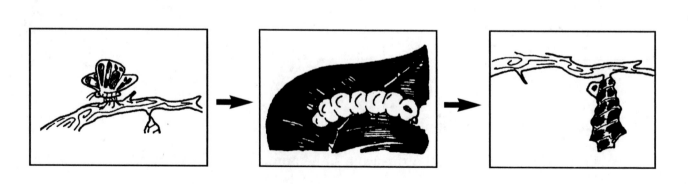

_____   _____   _____

Can you redraw this flow chart in the order it happens in nature? Try it!

How Does It Happen?

There are nine picture on this page that show steps that are used to make a doghouse. Cut them out and paste them on a separate piece of paper in the correct order. Use numbers or arrows to show the sequence.

BARNEY

Story Time!

Can you use your imagination to make a flow chart for a story? A story about a fierce dragon is started for you. Make up the rest of the story about this dragon. The last box is your ending. Write your words in the left boxes and draw some pictures in the right boxes that will go with your words.

Once upon a time, there was a very fierce dragon.	
The End	

In the Evening...

Here are five pictures that show things that many people do in the evening. Color them and cut them out.

Use the pictures to make a flow chart. Paste the pictures on a separate piece of large paper in the order you do them. Use arrows to show what picture is next.

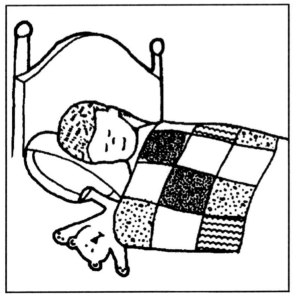

Organize Us!

Five friends are going on a picnic to the park. They are going to eat lunch and play games. This is what they need to bring.

tablecloth	apples
horseshoes	ball
lemonade	chips
napkins	cups
picnic basket	kite
sandwiches	bat
flying disc	plates
cookies	

Each friend needs to bring:

- one thing to eat
- one thing to help serve or carry lunch
- one thing to play with

Make a chart of the things the friends can bring

Our Picnic and Play Day			
Person	Food Item	Serving Item	Game Item
Jody			
Becky			
Carl			
Jessie			
Ernie			

Time Line

A *time line* is a way to show events that happen in the order they happen. You read time lines from left to right.

Read this time line. Then answer the questions.

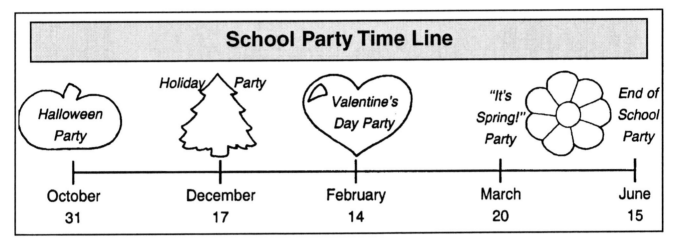

School Party Time Line

Halloween Party	Holiday Party	Valentine's Day Party	"It's Spring!" Party	End of School Party
October 31	December 17	February 14	March 20	June 15

1. What party came first this year? _____

2. What party came last this year? _____

3. What kind of party did the children have on March 20? _____

4. How many parties did the class have this year? _____

Make a time line using your birthday and the birthday dates of two other people in your class. Write the birthdays on the time line below.

name _____   name _____   name _____

___ date ___   ___ date ___   ___ date ___

It's History

Write these events from history in the right order on the time line.

In 1519, Ferdinand Magellan sailed from Spain, around the tip of South America, and across the Pacific Ocean. His crew continued around the Indian Ocean, the tip of Africa, and home to Spain.

In 1498, Vasco da Gama sailed from Portugal around the tip of Africa and reached India.

In 1491, Christopher Columbus sailed from Spain to the New World, landing the islands in the West Indies.

In 1497, John and Sebastian Cabot sailed from England to the New World, landing on the eastern coastline of Nova Scotia or Newfoundland.

1519

1497 1498

1492

explorer:

explorer:

explorer:

explorer:

Events in My Life

Work with your family to find the dates for very special events in your life. Some events might have just your age or a grade. Then choose the five events that you think are most important to you and write them on the time line below.

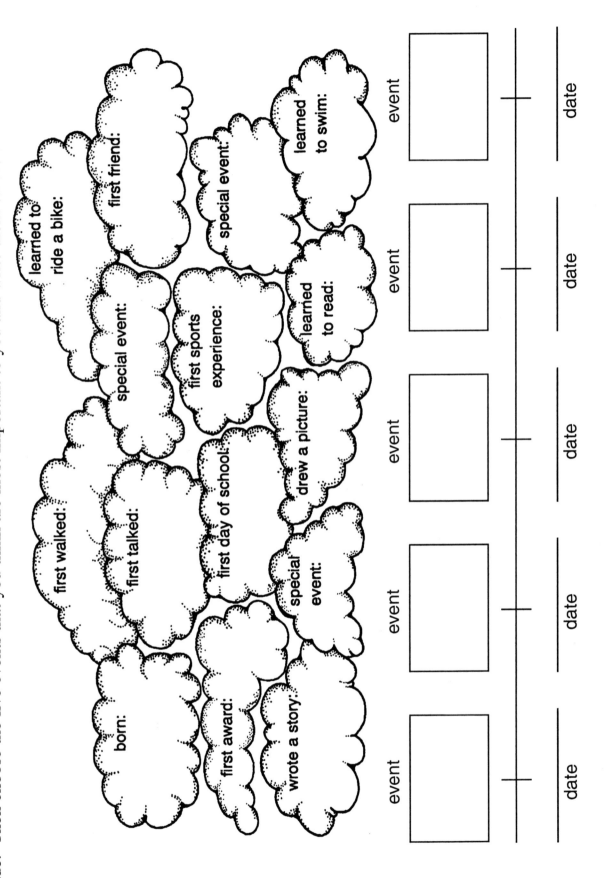

first friend:

learned to ride a bike:

special event:

learned to swim:

first sports experience:

learned to read:

first walked:

first talked:

first day of school:

drew a picture:

born:

first award:

wrote a story:

special event:

event _____ | date

event _____ | date

event _____ | date

event _____ | date

event _____ | date

Graphs

A *graph* is a visual tool that makes it easier for us to see information. There are many different types of graphs. In this book, we will learn about four of them. Here's what these types of graphs look like.

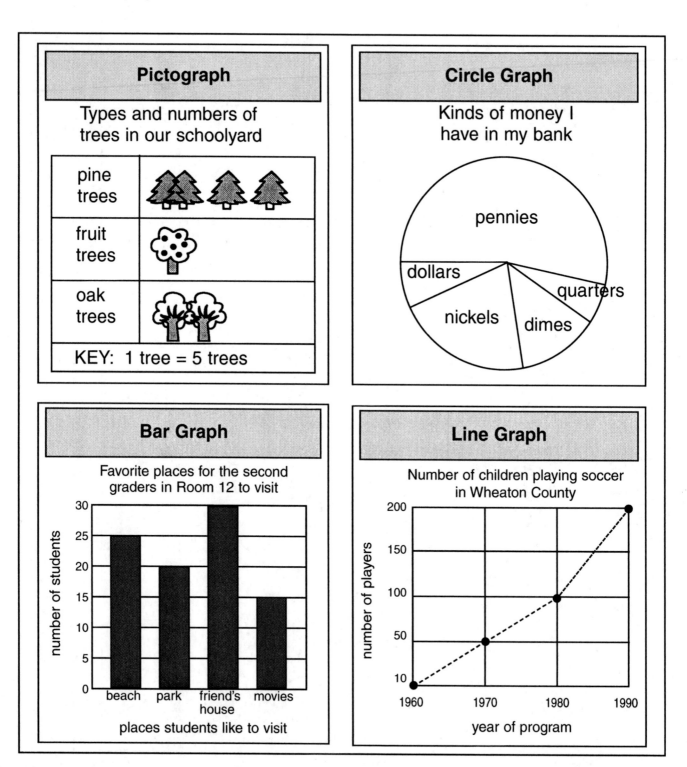

Use an encyclopedia, newspaper, magazine, or other resource to try to find one or more of these types of graphs.

Pictographs

One type of graph that gives us information is called a *pictograph*. In a pictograph, pictures are used instead of numbers.

Here is a pictograph that shows the number of fish caught each day at Canyon Lake.

Daily Fish Catch at Canyon Lake	
Sunday	🐟 🐟 🐟 🐟 🐟 🐟 🐟
Monday	🐟 🐟
Tuesday	🐟
Wednesday	🐟 🐟 🐟
Thursday	🐟 🐟
Friday	🐟 🐟 🐟 🐟
Saturday	🐟 🐟 🐟 🐟 🐟
KEY: 🐟 = 10 fish	

1. On what day were the most fish caught? _____
   How many fish were caught on this day? _____

2. On what day were 40 fish caught? _____

3. On what day were the fewest fish caught? _____

4. Were the same number of fish caught on Monday and Thursday? _____
   How many? _____

5. How many fish were caught on both Saturday and Sunday? _____
   (Add the two days together to get the total fish caught.)

Happy Birthday To You!

Your soccer coach needs to know in what months the team members have birthdays.

Can you look at this
pictograph and find out?

Birthdays of our Soccer Team

January	🧁	July	🧁
February	🧁	August	🧁 🧁
March		September	
April	🧁 🧁 🧁	October	
May	🧁 🧁	November	🧁
June		December	🧁

1. How many soccer players are on the team? _____

2. In what month were most of these soccer players born? _____

3. What months have no players' birthdays? _____

4. Does May or February have more birthdays? _____

5. What two months each have two birthdays? _____

_____

*Make a pictograph of the birthdays in your class!

Flowers

There are 25 people in Laura Smith's gardening club. She decided to find out the favorite flower of each club member. The results of what she found out are in this **pictograph.**

Favorite Flowers of the Greenville Garden Club

KEY: One flower equals one vote

1. What is the favorite of the Greenville Garden Club? _____

2. Did the members like lupines or violets more? _____

3. What two flowers got the same amount of votes? _____ and _____

4. How many people voted? _____

5. How many people in the club like violets most? _____

*What is your favorite flower? _____

What a Hungry Group!

Five good friends went on a picnic and ate a great deal of food and drank a lot of lemonade.

Read the **pictograph** to find out more about their picnic lunch!

What We Ate and Drank for Lunch	
sandwiches	🥪🥪🥪🥪🥪🥪🥪
apples	🍎🍎🍎🍎🍎
carrot sticks	//////////////// ////////////
bags of chips	🛍🛍🛍
cookies	🍪🍪🍪🍪🍪🍪🍪🍪 🍪🍪🍪🍪🍪🍪
glasses of lemonade	🥛🥛🥛🥛🥛🥛🥛🥛🥛

KEY: 1 pictures = 1 serving

1. How much of each of these things did the friends eat or drink?

   sandwiches _____ apples _____ carrot sticks _____

   bags of chips _____ cookies _____ glasses of lemonade _____

2. Did the friends eat more sandwiches or apples? _____

3. Did they eat more carrot sticks or cookies? _____

4. Was there enough lemonade for each friend to have 2 glasses? _____

We Can Do It!

Mrs. Hennesy's class is planning a trip to the city zoo. All student must raise their own money for the $5.00 zoo entrance fee.

Read the **pictograph** to find out how the students earned money for their trip. Then answer the questions below the graph.

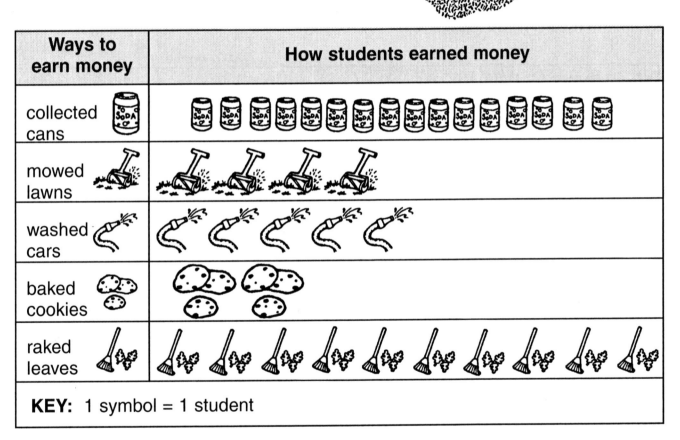

1. How many students earned money washing cars? _____

2. What kind of thing did **most** students do to earn money for the trip? _____

3. How many students earned money collecting cans for recycling? _____

4. What kind of thing did the **least** amount of students do to raise money? _____

5. How many students earned money mowing lawns? _____

*What do **you** do to earn extra money? _____

Popcorn Time!

At the school carnival, the scouts earned money for their troop projects by selling popcorn. Each scout worked for an hour and kept track of how many bags of popcorn were sold that hour. Here is the list the troop members made of their sales.

1:00 – 2:00 : 5 bags	4:00 – 5:00 : 15 bags
2:00 – 3:00 : 25 bags	5:00 – 6:00 : 5 bags
3:00 – 4:00 : 30 bags	6:00 – 7:00 : 40 bags

Make a **pictograph** of the popcorn sales by the hour. Check the key to find out what symbol to use.

Troop 81 Popcorn Sales	
1:00 – 2:00	
2:00 – 3:00	
3:00 – 4:00	
4:00 – 5:00	
5:00 – 6:00	
6:00 – 7:00	
KEY: = 5 bags of popcorn	

Circle Graphs

One type of graph that gives us information is called a **circle graph**. In a circle graph, you can show how things are divided into the parts of a whole.

Read this circle graph of where Derek spends the hours in one day.

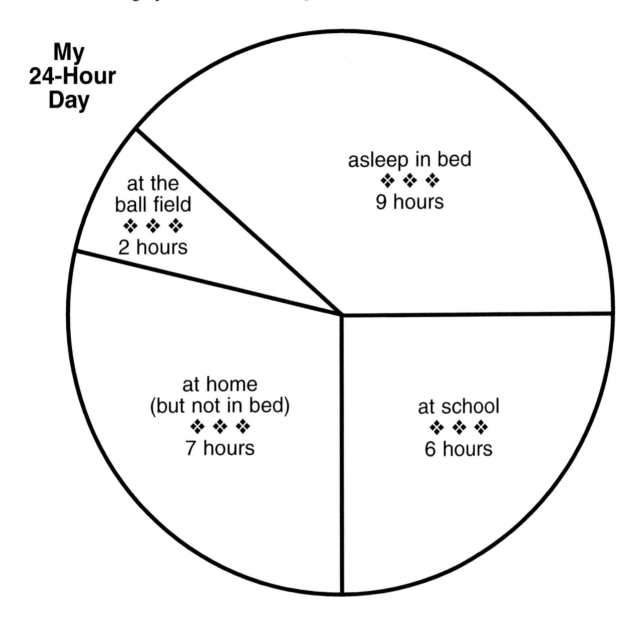

- Color the place Derek spends 6 hours a day red.

- Color Derek's sleeping time blue.

- Color the time Derek spends on the ball field green.

- Color Derek's non-sleep time at home yellow.

- On the back of this paper, write some of the things you think Derek might do at home in 7 hours.

Under the Big Top

The circus has come to your town and you want to know as much as you can about the kinds of animals that are under the circus tent. You count them and record what you find out on a circle graph.

Kinds of Animals Under the Big Top

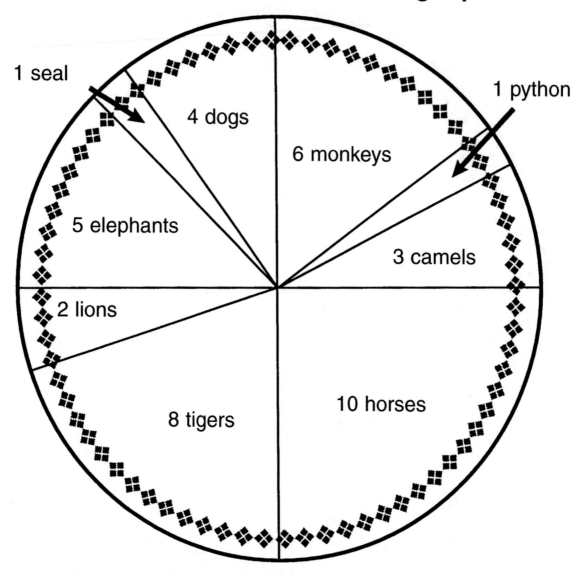

1 seal

1 python

4 dogs

6 monkeys

5 elephants

3 camels

2 lions

10 horses

8 tigers

1. How many animals are "under the Big Top"? _____

2. Are there more tigers or monkeys? _____

3. What animals are the only ones of their kind? _____

4. What animal do you find most at the circus? _____

5. What animals in this circus might you see in your neighborhood?

_____

A Week of Weather

Use these symbols to keep a record of a week of weather.

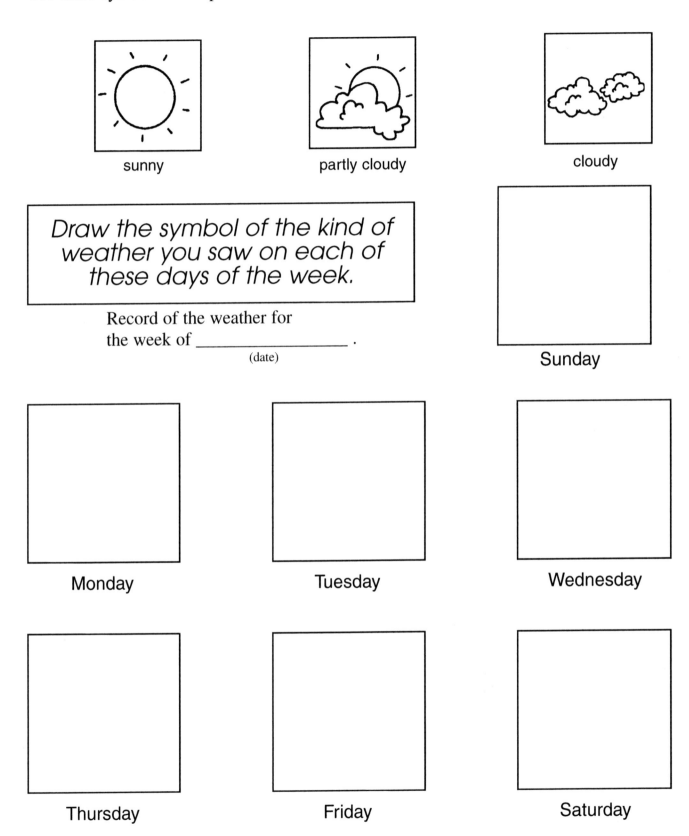

sunny

partly cloudy

cloudy

Draw the symbol of the kind of weather you saw on each of these days of the week.

Record of the weather for the week of _____ .
(date)

Sunday

Monday

Tuesday

Wednesday

Thursday

Friday

Saturday

Graph this weather information you recorded on the circle graph on page 46.

A Weather Circle Graph

Use the key below to color this circle graph according to the information you collected on page 45. **Put all slices of the same kind of weather next to each other so you can color a block of color.**

Then answer the questions.

A Week of Weather for the Week of

_____

(date)

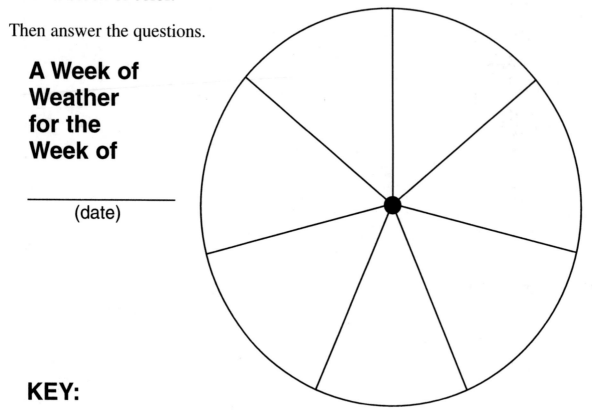

KEY:

☼ = [yellow]   ⛅ = [blue]   ☁☁ = [gray]

1. How many days were:

   sunny? _____ partly cloudy? _____ cloudy? _____

2. Was the week more sunny or partly cloudy? _____

3. Was the week more sunny or cloudy? _____

4. Was the week more partly cloudy or cloudy? _____

5. Did you like the weather this week? _____ Why? _____

_____

Slice It Up!

In a **circle graph**, all the parts must add up to be a whole. Think of the parts like pieces that add up to one whole pie. Look at these pies and how they are divided into pieces.

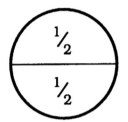
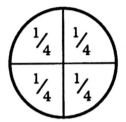

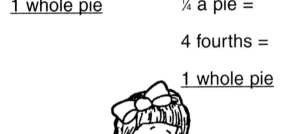

½ a pie +

½ a pie =

2 halves =

<u>1 whole pie</u>

¼ a pie +

¼ a pie +

¼ a pie +

¼ a pie =

4 fourths =

<u>1 whole pie</u>

⅛ a pie +

⅛ a pie +

⅛ a pie +

⅛ a pie +

⅛ a pie +

⅛ a pie +

⅛ a pie +

⅛ a pie =

8 eighths =

<u>1 whole pie</u>

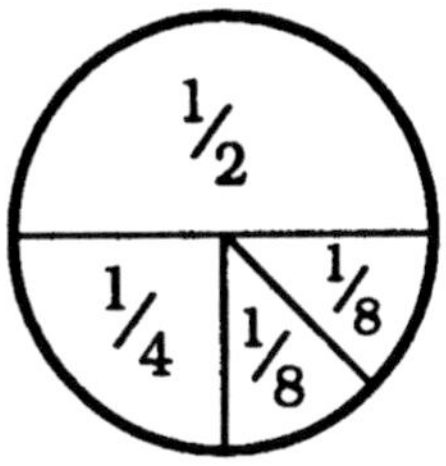

½ a pie +

¼ a pie +

⅛ a pie +

⅛ a pie =

1 half +

1 fourth +

2 eighths =

<u>1 whole pie</u>

Make a circle graph to show how much pie a family ate. Here is the information you will need.

Mother ate ¼ of the pie.

Sister ate ¼ of the pie.

Father ate ¼ of the pie.

Brother ate ⅛ of the pie.

Grandma ate ⅛ of the pie.

PIE MY FAMILY ATE

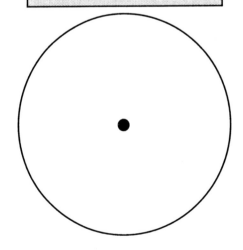

KEY:

sister = orange	grandma = red
mother = pink	brother = yellow father = blue

Bar Graphs

One type of graph that gives us information is called a bar graph. A bar graph shows us many different types of things by the height or length of the bars.

A single bar graph is one type of bar graph. Questions that ask what kind, what place, how much, how long, and how many can be answered by using a single bar graph.

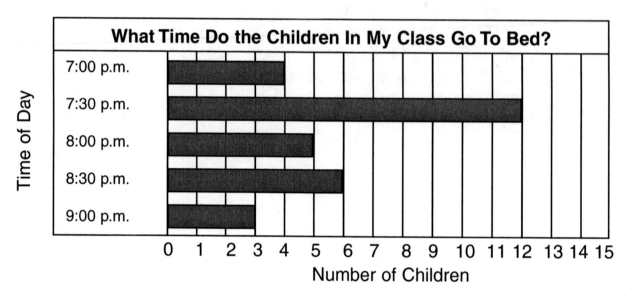

A **double bar graph** (or **multiple bar graph**) is another type of bar graph. It is used to compare two or more things.

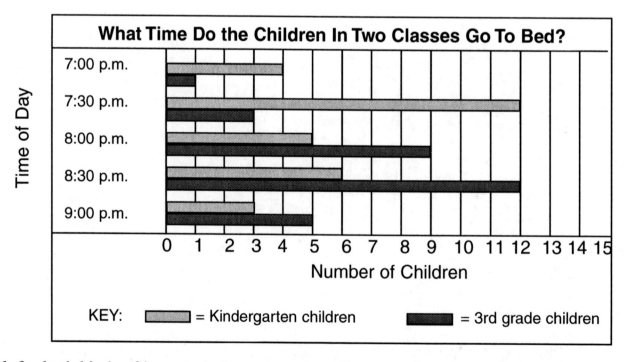

*Look for both kinds of bar graphs in an encyclopedia, magazines, newspaper, or other resource. Share what you find with your class.

Choose Your Color!

Mrs. Briddle asked her class of 28 students to vote for their favorite color. This is what they said.

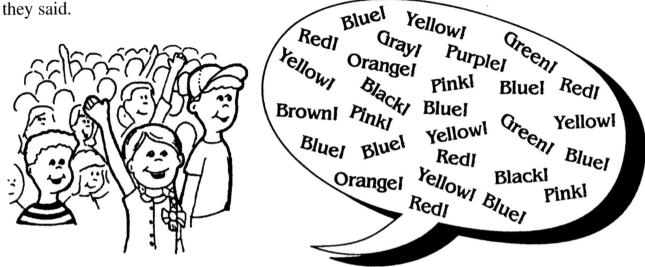

Count the votes for each color and write the number on these lines. It might help you to cross out each color after you count it.

red: _____   pink: _____   blue: _____   yellow: _____   green: _____

brown: _____   orange: _____   black: _____   purple: _____   gray: _____

Write the name of each color under its correct number on the graph. Then color the bar to match the color name. Some colors are done for you.

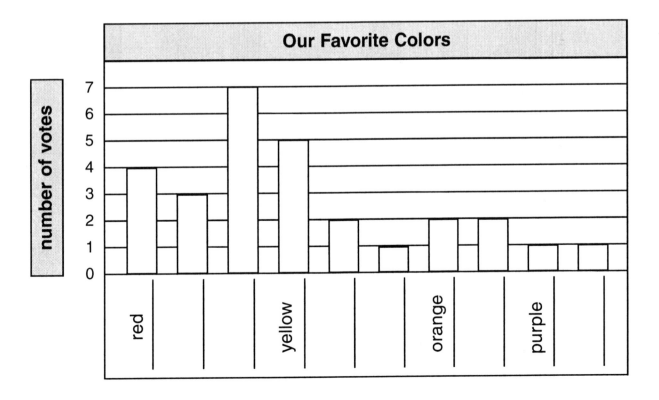

Which Class?

The classes at Barnsdale Elementary School kept a **bar graph** of the number of books each grade read for a week.

Study this bar graph of their reading and answer the questions below.

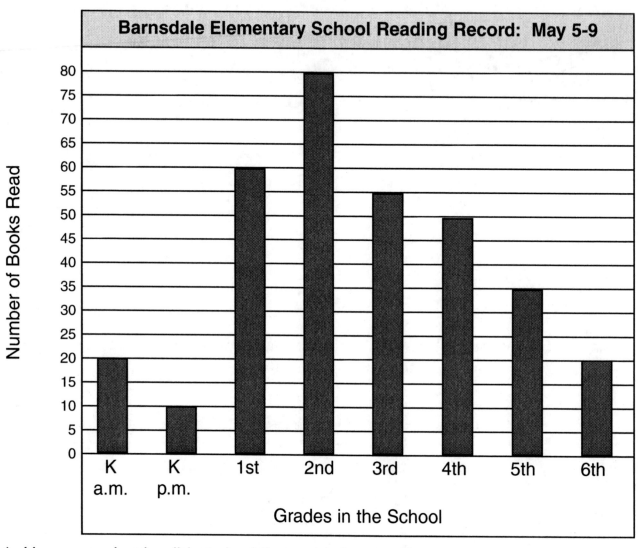

1. How many books did each of these grades read?

   K a.m. _____1st _____3rd_____5th _____

   K p.m. _____2nd _____4th_____6th _____

2. Which grade read the most books? _____

3. What two grades read the same number of books? _____

   Which books do you think are longer, the books kindergartners read or the

   books sixth graders read? _____

*How many books can you read in a week? Try it! _____

Through the Years

A bar graph can give you an easy way to see how things **compare**.

This bar graph shows you the amount of rain three different cities got on the same day in three different years.

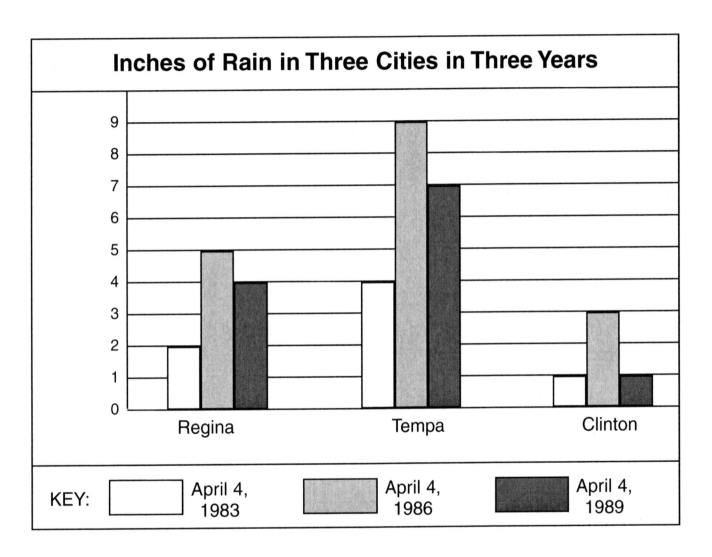

1. What city was the wettest city in all three years? _____

2. What city was the driest in all three years? _____

3. How many inches of rain fell in Regina in April of 1986? _____

4. What city had the same inches of rain in two different years? _____

   _____How many inches? _____

5. What year had the most rain in all three cities? _____

Our Favorite Things

Joanna took a survey to find out how two different age groups liked five different things. There were ten children in each of the age groups she asked. Here is what she found out.

Question: Which of these toys or games do you like best?

6 year-olds	10 year-olds
remote-control cars – 1	remote-control cars – 2
video games – 2	video games – 1
soccer – 2	soccer – 4
board games – 2	board games – 2
stuffed animals – 3	stuffed animals – 3

Put the information Joanna collected in a bar graph. Some of the graph has been done for you.

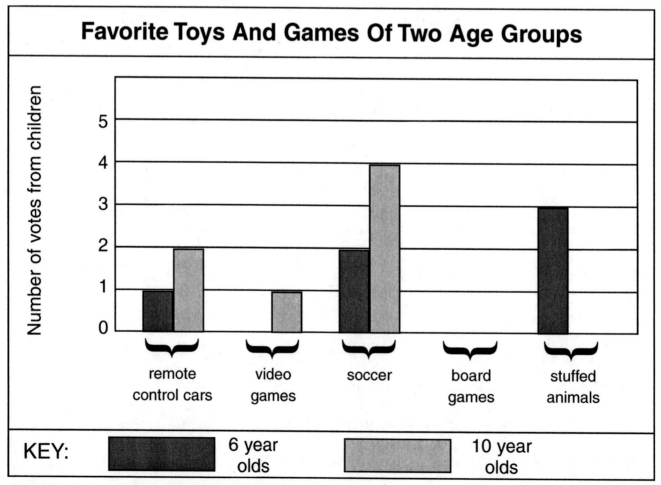

Draw the Bars!

Draw the bars to show how many hours a week five children spend playing outside or watching television.

Here is the information you will need to make your bar graph.

Barbara – outside: 8 television: 12

Joe – outside: 6 television: 20

Jennifer – outside: 14 television 10

Michael – outside: 20 television 6

Sandra – outside: 16 television: 10

Use the colors in the key to make your bar graph.

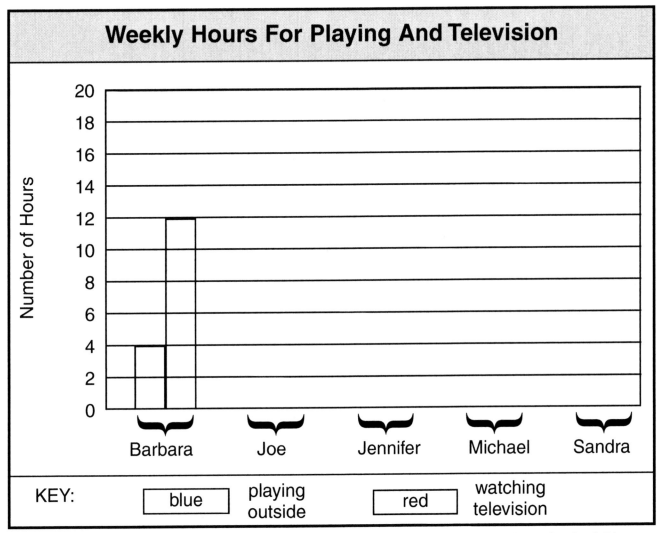

Line Graphs

One type of graph that gives us information is called a *line graph*. A line graph uses dots and lines to show how things change and compare.

Mr. Dean gives five homework assignments each week. He asks his students to graph how many assignments they turn in each week. Here is one of his student's graphs of a six week period.

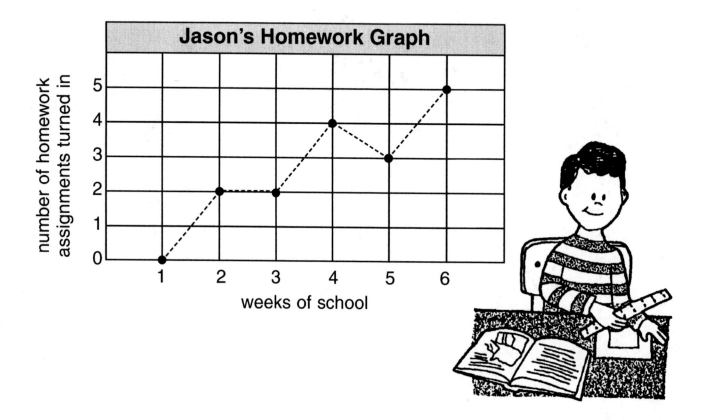

1. How many homework assignments did Jason turn in during each of these weeks?

   week 1 _____ week 3 _____ week 5 _____

   week 2 _____ week 4 _____ week 6 _____

2. What week was his best "homework turned in" week? _____

3. What week was his worst "homework turned in" week? _____

4. Did Jason turn in more homework in the first few weeks or the last few weeks on the graph? _____

*Keep a graph of our homework assignments, too!

Connect the Dots

Mr. Dean has two students who have not made graphs of their homework. He wants you to make their graphs. Don't forget to connect the dots!

Here is the information you will need for Susan's graph.

week 1 __3__   week 3 __2__   week 5 __3__

week 2 __3__   week 4 __4__   week 6 __4__

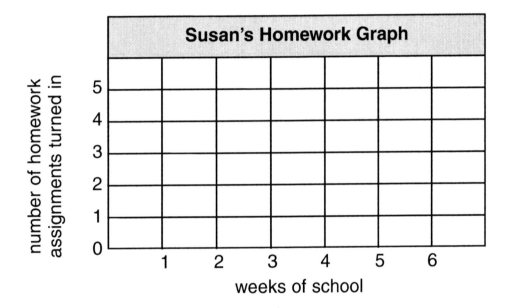

Here is the information you will need for Brian's graph.

week 1 __4__   week 3 __5__   week 5 __5__

week 2 __5__   week 4 __4__   week 6 __5__

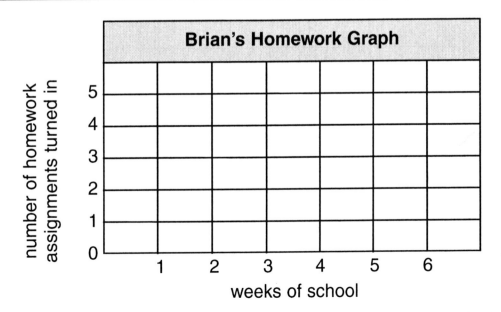

       TCM 168 – Beginning Charts, Graphs, & Diagrams

My Pet, Mr. Snuffles

Mr. Snuffles is a very unusual pet. He has purple skin, yellow eyes, six legs, and a tail shaped like a smile. He is also a very fast grower.

Graph these figures and you'll see what I mean.

The first week I had him, he weighed 5 pounds.

The second week I had him, he weighed 10 pounds.

The third week I had him, he weighed 15 pounds.

The fourth week I had him, he weighed 20 pounds.

The fifth week I had him, he weighed 25 pounds.

I have had him for six weeks now and he weights 30 pounds.

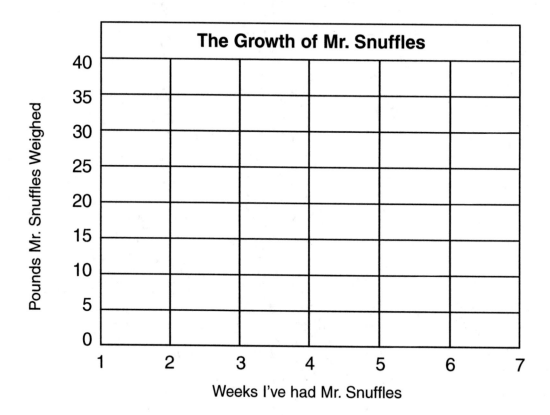

How much do you think Mr. Snuffles will weigh on the seventh week?

_____Graph your guess.

How do you know? _____

_____

Draw a picture of Mr. Snuffles on the back of this paper.

Compare!

Sometimes two different things can be compared on the same line graph. A different color or type of line is used for each thing you want to compare. Graphs with more than one type or color of line are called **double line graphs**.

Here is a comparison of the number of hours Tony spent outside during two weeks of the same year.

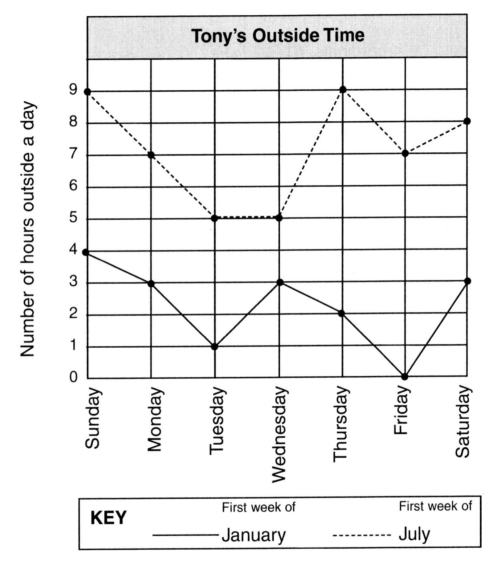

1. How many hours did Tony spend outside on these days?

a. Tuesday, January _____ b. Saturday, July _____

c. Wednesday, July _____ d. Sunday, January _____

e. Monday, January _____ f. Friday, July _____

2. Why do you think Tony spent more time outside in July than he did in January? _____

Draw the Lines!

Carol and Jessie kept track of how many bluejays and how many cardinals came to their bird feeder in one week.

Here is their information. Graph the number of birds that they saw each day.			
Sunday	7 cardinals 10 bluejays	Thursday	2 cardinals 5 bluejays
Monday	4 cardinals 6 bluejays	Friday	4 cardinals 6 bluejays
Tuesday	12 cardinals 15 bluejays	Saturday	11 cardinals 14 bluejays
Wednesday	9 cardinals 11 bluejays		

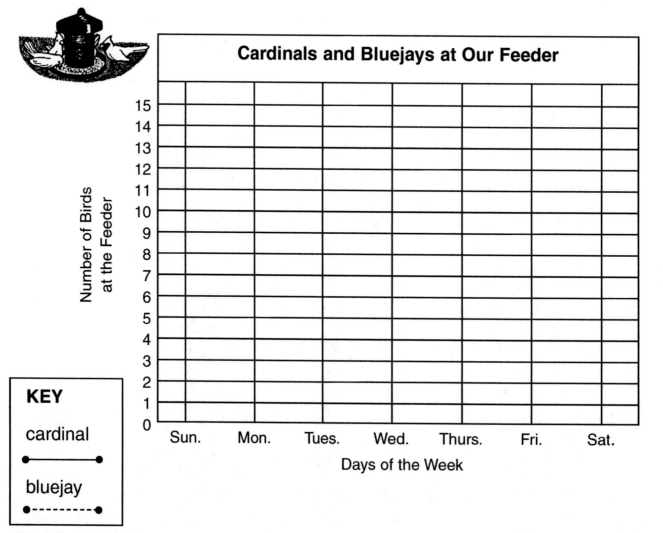

Cardinals and Bluejays at Our Feeder

Number of Birds at the Feeder

15
14
13
12
11
10
9
8
7
6
5
4
3
2
1
0

Sun.   Mon.   Tues.   Wed.   Thurs.   Fri.   Sat.

Days of the Week

KEY

cardinal
●————————●

bluejay
●- - - - - - - -●

Graph Game

There are some letters of the alphabet hidden in these three graphs. Can you make the dots and draw the lines to find them?

Directions:

1. Begin on the left side of the graph.

2. Match the number in each pair with the number at the bottom. Match the letter in each pair with the letter on the left side of the graph.

3. Mark all the pairs with dots and connect the lines.

4. Write the name of the mystery letter on the line next to the graph.

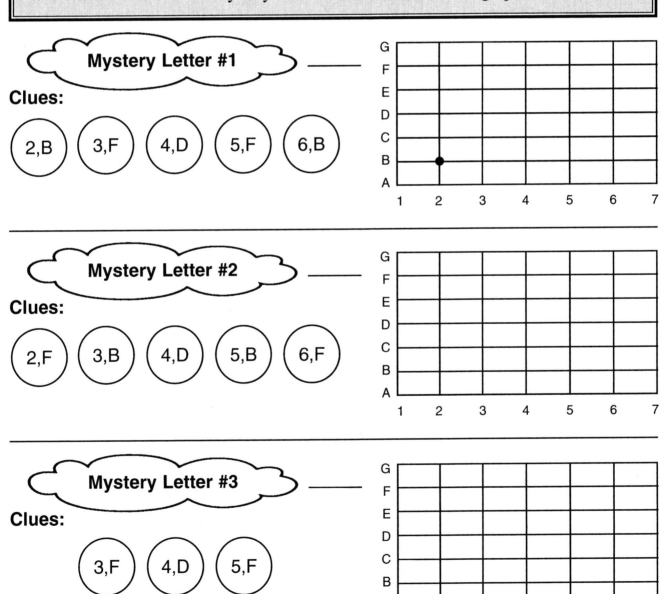

Mystery Letter #1 _____

Clues:

(2,B) (3,F) (4,D) (5,F) (6,B)

Mystery Letter #2 _____

Clues:

(2,F) (3,B) (4,D) (5,B) (6,F)

Mystery Letter #3 _____

Clues:

(3,F) (4,D) (5,F)

Diagrams

Sometimes pictures can show you the parts of things. These pictures are called *diagrams*. In a diagram, arrows and labels help you identify the parts.

> *Study this diagram of a horse. Then answer the questions at the bottom of the page.*

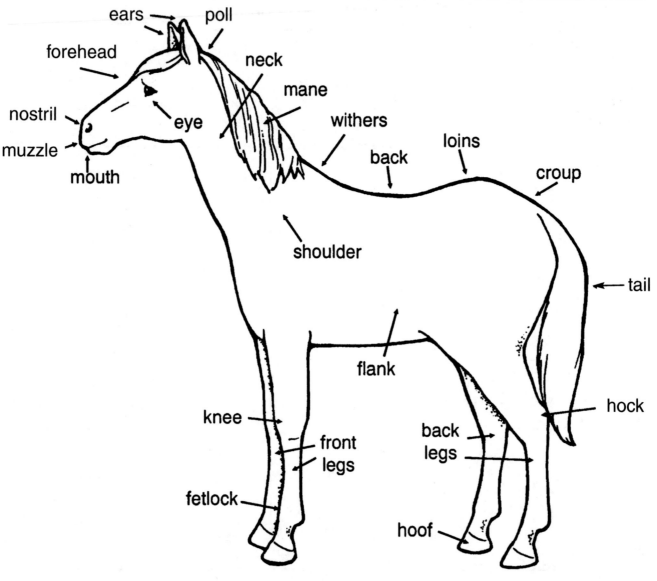

1. On what part of the horse is the hock? _____

2. Near what part of the horse is the poll? _____

3. What labels of the horse's body could you use to label the parts of your
   body? _____

   _____

   _____

Let's Compare

How big is the sun?

How does the Earth compare in size to the sun and other planets?

Look at the diagram and answer the questions below.

True or False

1. _____ Mercury and Pluto are the smallest planets.

2. _____ The Earth and Mars are almost exactly the same size.

3. _____ Jupiter is the largest of the nine planets.

4. _____ The size of the sun is enormous when compared to the planets.

5. _____ Jupiter, Saturn, Uranus, and Neptune are larger than Earth.

Sizes in Our Solar System

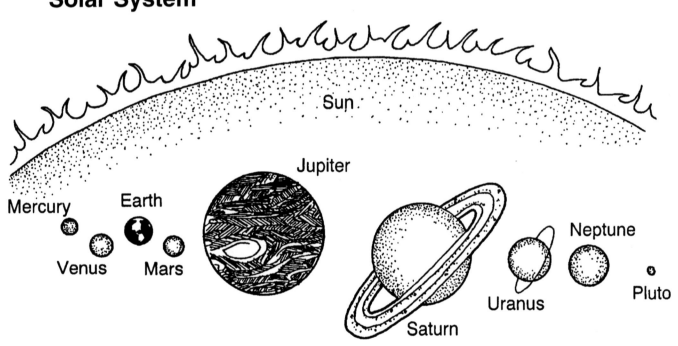

* Look in a reference book to find the size of the sun and the nine planets. Write the information you find on this diagram.

Look and Label

This is a diagram of a plant of wheat. But someone forgot to label the parts! Use a reference book to help you label the parts of this wheat plant. Use the words in the box to help you.

roots	stem	head
leaves	beard	kernel

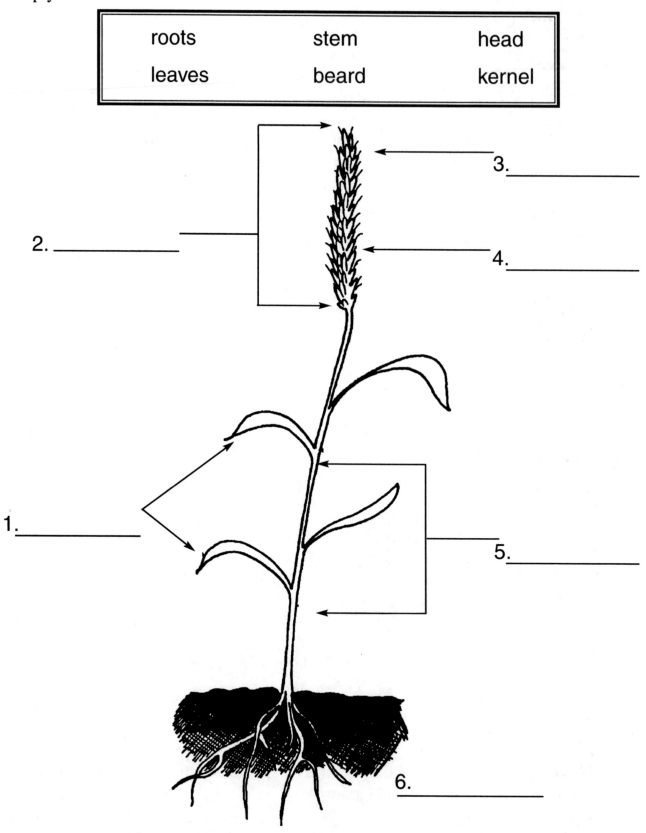

2. _____

3. _____

4. _____

1. _____

5. _____

6. _____

Research

Use an encyclopedia or other resource to help you label this diagram of a baseball field.

Some Parts of a Baseball Field for You to Label		
first base	batter's boxes	infield
second base	pitcher's plate (or mound)	outfield
third base		left field
home base	backstop	center field
catcher's box	foul lines	right field

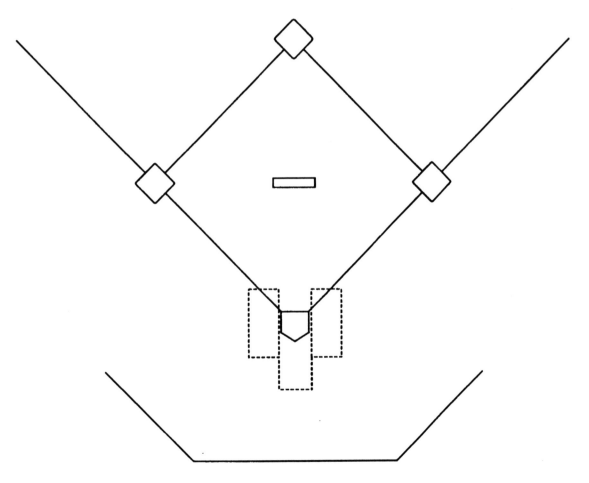

Color the infield light brown and the outfield green.

Cutaway Diagrams

Sometimes a diagram can show you what something would look like if you sliced it open. Diagrams that show you how the inside of something looks are called *cutaway diagrams.*

A Cutaway Diagram of a Blueberry Pie

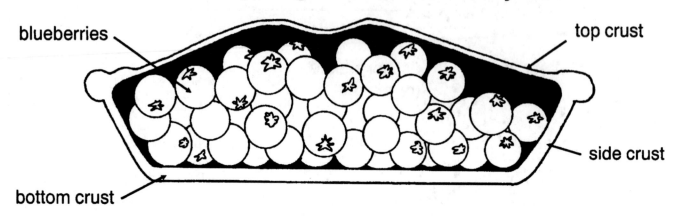

blueberries

top crust

side crust

bottom crust

Draw a cutaway diagram of each of these types of food. You may use a "real" slice to help you draw your picture.

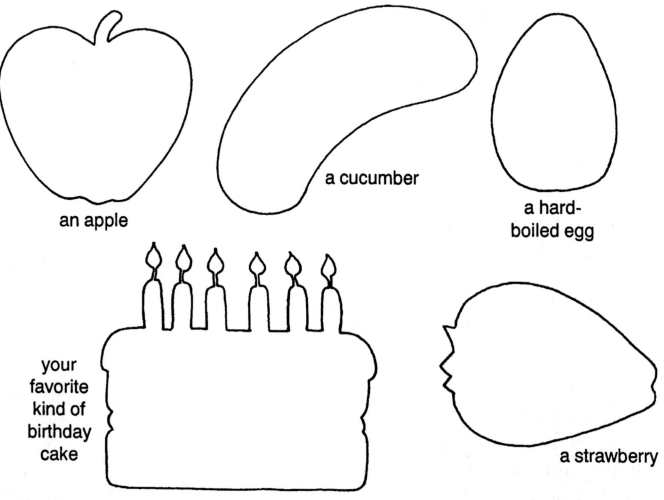

an apple

a cucumber

a hard-
boiled egg

your
favorite
kind of
birthday
cake

a strawberry

Ant City!

Have you ever wondered what it looks like inside an ant hill? You will get an idea from studying this **cutaway diagram.**

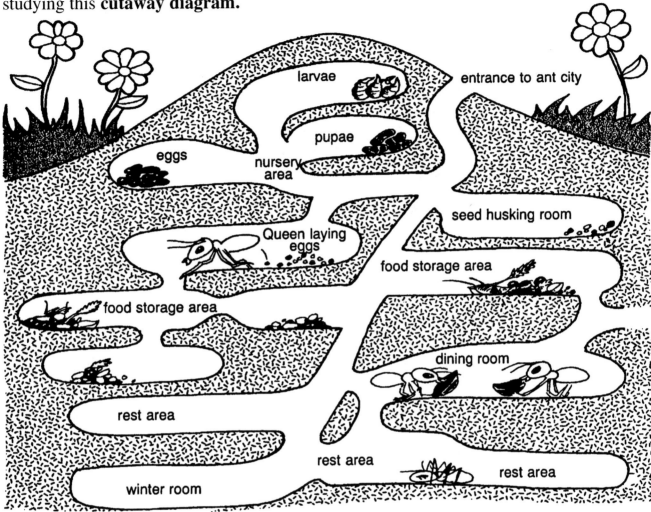

Use this color key to color the rooms of this ant hill.		

yellow	nursery area (eggs, pupae, larvae)	blue	rest area	orange	food storage area
purple	winter room	green	seed husking room	red	dining room

Think about it: Why do you think the nursery is at the top of the ant city and the winter room is at the bottom? _____

_____

Guessing Game!

Look at the cutaway diagrams on this page. Can you guess what they are?

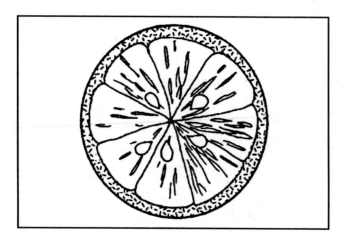

1. _____

2. _____

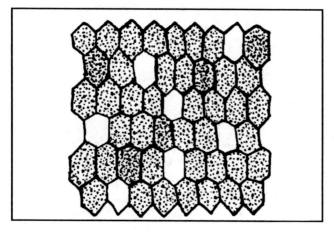

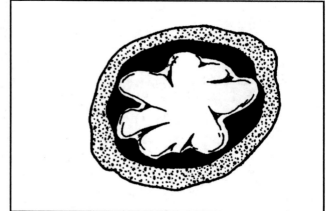

3. _____

4. _____

You draw a cutaway diagram of something. Show it to someone else in your room. Can he or she guess what it is?

5. _____

Venn Diagrams

A **Venn diagram** is a type of diagram that uses circles to show how things are related to each other. The overlapping parts of the circles show what things the circles have in common.

Look at this diagram of the activities of two kindergarten classes that share the same room.

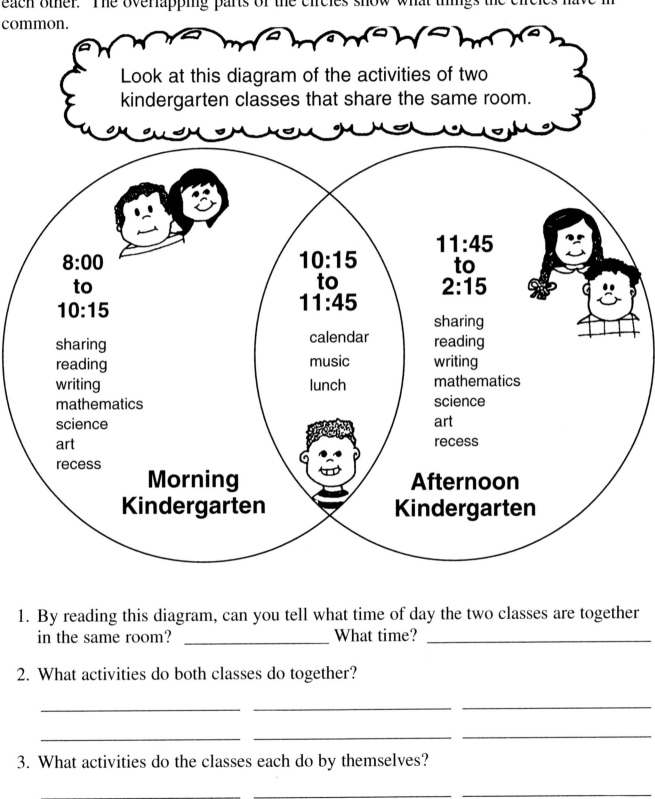

8:00 to 10:15

sharing
reading
writing
mathematics
science
art
recess

Morning Kindergarten

10:15 to 11:45

calendar
music
lunch

11:45 to 2:15

sharing
reading
writing
mathematics
science
art
recess

Afternoon Kindergarten

1. By reading this diagram, can you tell what time of day the two classes are together in the same room? _____ What time? _____

2. What activities do both classes do together?

_____   _____   _____

_____   _____   _____

3. What activities do the classes each do by themselves?

_____   _____   _____

_____   _____   _____

_____

Games

There are many games you can play that use a ball. Write the names of four games that use a ball.

1. _____ 2. _____

3. _____ 4. _____

You can play some ball games with just a ball. You do not have to have any other equipment to play the game. Some ball games that can be played without equipment are catch, kickball, soccer, and football.

You need a ball and at least one piece of equipment to play some ball games. What do you need besides a ball for these games?

basketball _____

tetherball _____

baseball _____

tennis _____

volleyball _____

Make a Venn Diagram for two ball sports. Write the names of the sports on the top of each circle. Write the tings that are the same for both in the center. Write the things that are different in the outer circles.

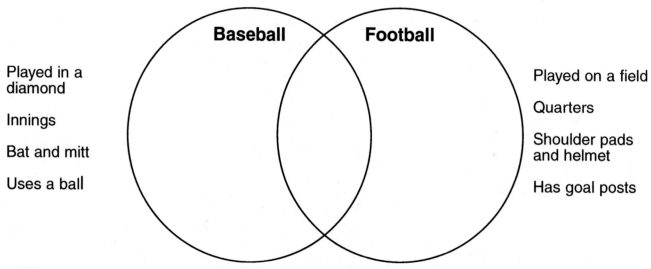

Played in a
diamond

Innings

Bat and mitt

Uses a ball

Baseball   **Football**

Played on a field

Quarters

Shoulder pads
and helmet

Has goal posts

Animals, Animals, Animals!

Write the name of each of these animals where it belongs in the diagram below.

lizard
(reptile)

cow
(mammal)

butterfly
(insect)

ant
(insect)

bee
(insect)

lion
(mammal)

turtle
(reptile)

dog
(mammal)

elephant
(mammal)

snake
(reptile)

grasshopper
(insect)

crocodile
(reptile)

Animals

Reptile	Insect	Mammal

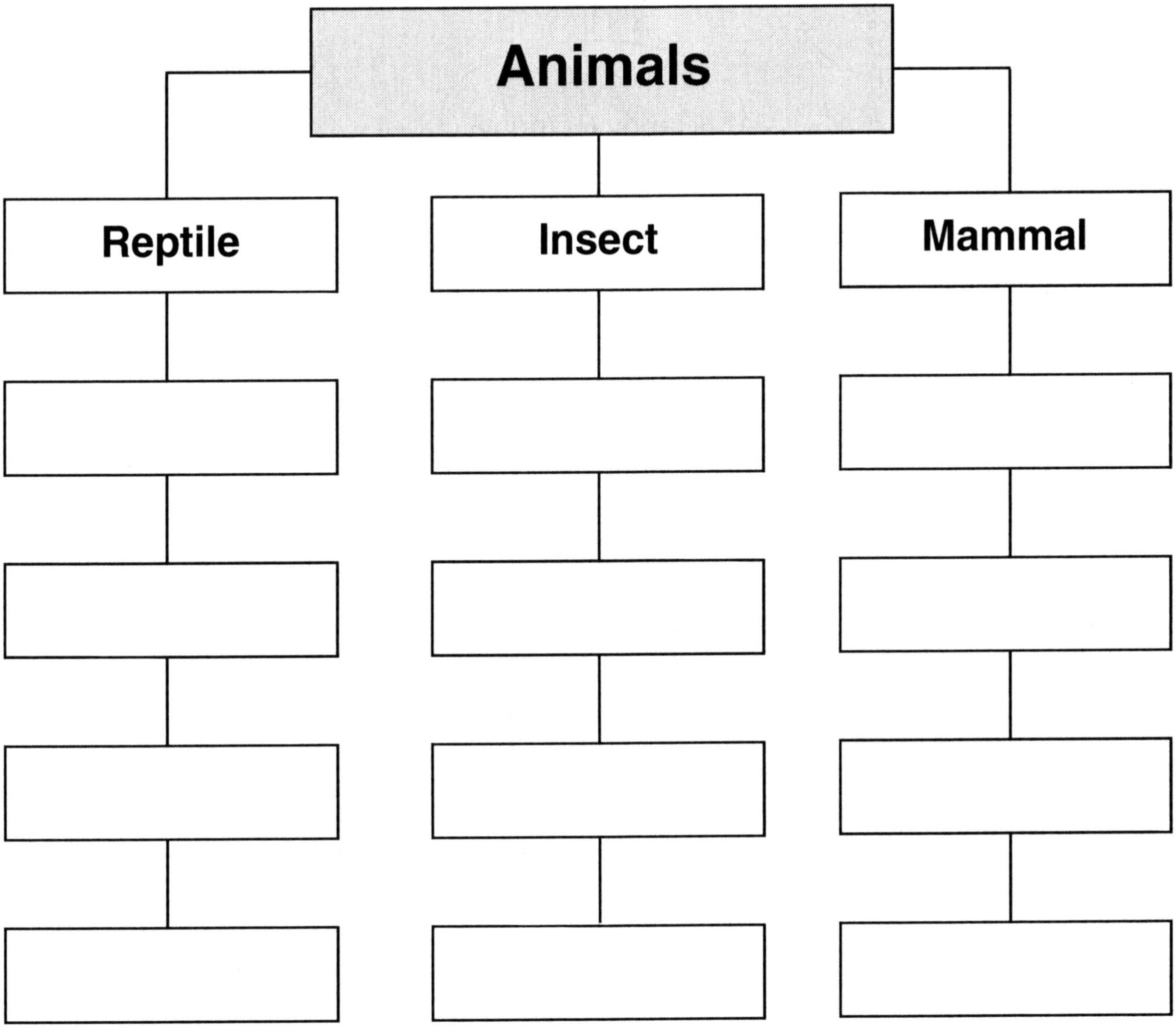

Mind Mapping

You can make a diagram of your ideas. A diagram of ideas is called a **mind map**.

Look at the mind map Nick made for his birthday party.

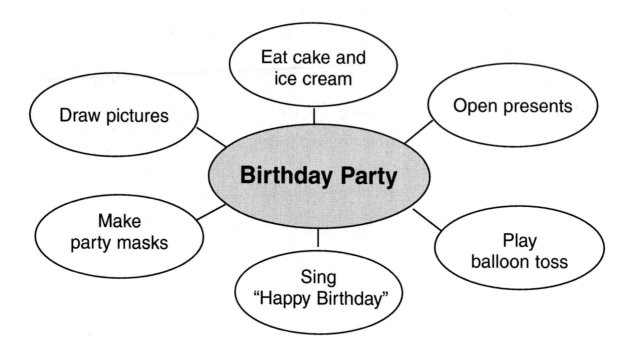

Make a mind map of six things you can do on a rainy day

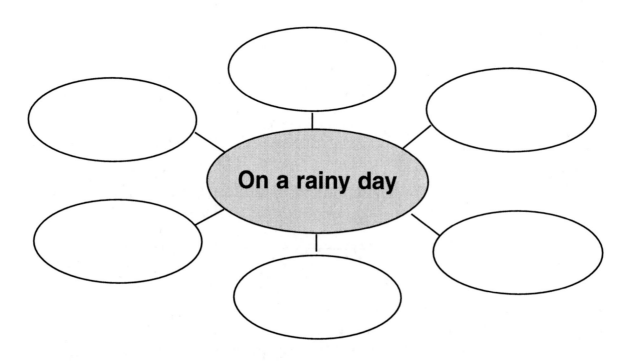

My Story Plan

It's time to write a story!

Think of a character that would make a great hero. Then complete the story diagram on this page.

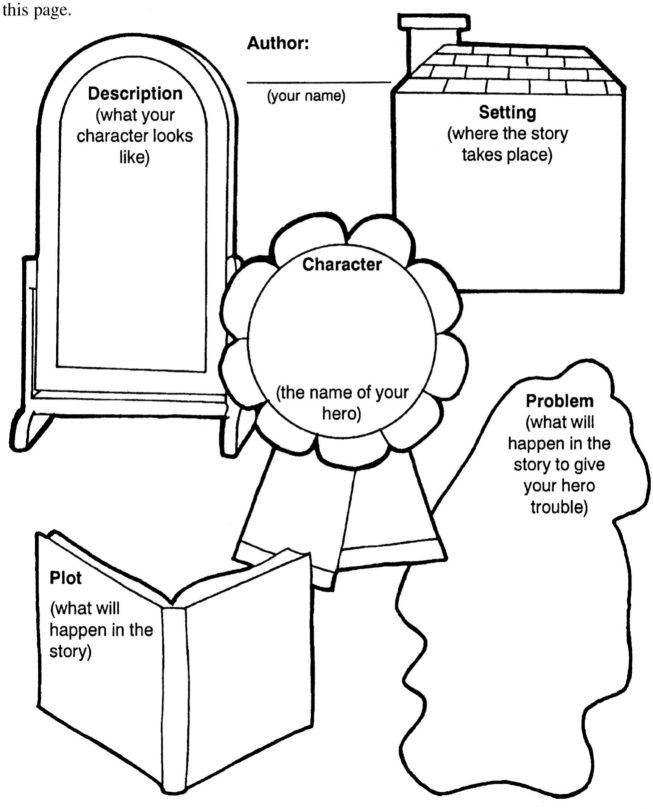

Author:

_____
(your name)

Description
(what your character looks like)

Setting
(where the story takes place)

Character

(the name of your hero)

Problem
(what will happen in the story to give your hero trouble)

Plot
(what will happen in the story)

ME!

It's time to think about yourself!

1. Write your name in the center of the mind map.

2. Write the things you do well in the circles.

3. Write the things you do not do well in the squares. (You may add more circles or squares if you need them.)

4. Put a star next to everything that makes you feel proud of yourself.

5. Draw a circle around the things you could do better if you practiced.

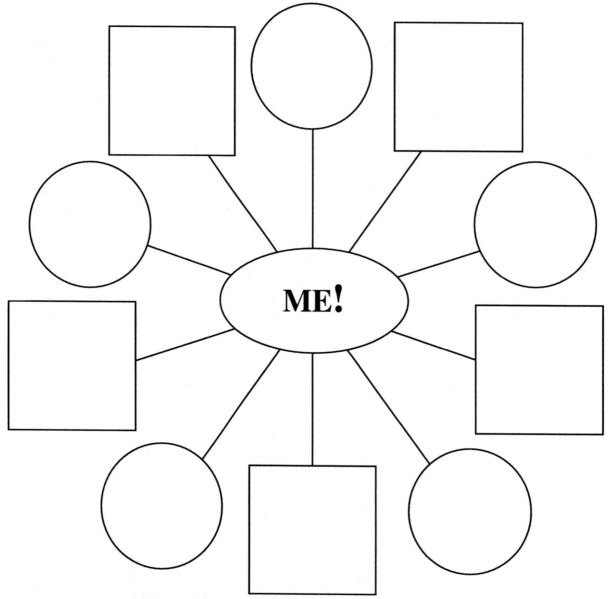

Do this again in one month and see if anything changes.

Chart Form

Use this chart form for weekly activities.

Activity	Sun.	Mon.	Tues.	Wed.	Thurs.	Fri.	Sat.
1.							
2.							
3.							
4.							
5.							
6.							
7.							
8.							
9.							
10.							

Distance Chart Form

Use this chart form for making a distance chart. (See pages 24 and 25.)

Distance Chart computed in _____ (miles or kilometers).	1.	2.	3.	4.	5.	6.	7.
2.		▨					
3.			▨				
4.				▨			
5.					▨		
6.						▨	
7.							▨
8.							

Bar Graph Form

Use this form for a bar graph.

KEY:

Line Graph Form

Use this form for a line graph or graph game.

KEY:

Answer Key

Charts, Graphs, Diagrams

p. 4

You might find it easier for your children to understand each of the graphics on this page if you reproduced them on the board in a much larger size.

P. 5

1. 4
2. no
3. no
4. 2
5. 1
6. 3 inches
7. plain circle

P. 6

Answers will vary. Check for appropriate responses.

P. 7

Tyrannosaurus Rex

P. 9

1. 1¢
2. 5¢
3. 10¢
4. 5 – 1
5. 2 – 1
6. 10 – 1
7. 5¢ or a nickel
8. 10¢ or a dime
9. 10¢ or a dime

P. 10

Answers are given from the top and left to right.

17, 17, 6, 16, 9, 21, 10, 4

P. 11

1. reading – 6
2. science and physical education
3. yes – mathematics
4. yes
5. yes

P. 13

Bambi – 5

Lady and the Tramp – 1

Heroes in a Halfshell – 4

Superman – 2

The Land Before Time – 7

E.T. – 4

Oliver & Company – 1

The Karate Kid – 3

Transformers – 2

Cinderella – 2

1. The Land Before Time – 7
2. Bambi
3. E.T. and Heroes in a Halfshell

P. 15

1. yes – starting on page 3
2. 11, 41, 53
3. parrots, lizards
4. Chapter 1, 5
5. yes, 59

P. 16

Dinosaurs by Ty Rex

1. Apatosaurus p. 3
2. Pteranodon p. 8
3. Stegosaurus p. 13
4. Triceratops p. 18
5. Tyrannosaurus p. 23

P. 18

Check page 17 for the correctness of answers.

P. 20

Check page 19 for the correctness of answers. Checking as a class activity is a great teaching tool for this chart.

P. 23

Check as a class activity. Use page 22 to help you.

P. 24

1. 108
2. 30
3. 13
4. 135
5. 9
6. 3
7. 104

P. 25

1. Boston

   Chicago

   Los Angeles

   Montreal

   New York City

   Seattle

2. a. 2873

   b. 963

   c. 2815

   d. 828

   e. 206

   f. 1131

3. a. Seattle

   b. Montreal

   c. Boston

4. a. New York City

   b. Seattle

   c. New York City

Answer Key *(cont.)*

P. 26

1. week 1
2. 2 cm
3. week 5 and week 6 – week 6 was measured on a Thursday instead of a Monday
4. 26 cm

P. 27

1. mother
2. sister
3. father

P. 28

1. caterpillar, cocoon, butterfly

P. 29

Correct as a class activity.

P. 32

Check as a class activity.

P. 33

1. Halloween Party
2. End of School Party
3. "It's Spring!" party
4. 5

P. 34

1. Columbus
2. Cabot
3. Vasco da Gamma
4. Magellan

P. 35

Share these event time line as a class.

P. 37

1. Sunday, 60 fish
2. Friday
3. Tuesday
4. yes – 20 fish
5. 110 fish

P. 38

1. 12 players
2. April
3. March, June, September, and October
4. May
5. May and August

P. 39

1. rose
2. lupines
3. tulips and daisies
4. 25
5. 1 person

P. 40

1. 7 sandwiches, 5 apples, 28 carrot sticks, 3 bags of chips, 19 cookies, 10 glasses of lemonade
2. sandwiches
3. carrot sticks
4. yes

P. 41

1. 5
2. collected cans
3. 16
4. baked cookies
5. 4

P. 44

1. 40 animals
2. tigers
3. python, seal
4. horses
5. probably dogs, possibly horses

P. 46

Check as a class activity.

P. 47

P. 49

red: 4

pink: 3

blue: 7

yellow: 5

green: 2

brown: 1

orange: 2

black: 2

purple: 1

gray: 1

P. 50

1. K a.m.: 20
   K p.m.: 10
   1st: 60
   2nd: 80
   3rd: 55
   4th: 50
   5th: 35
   6th: 20
2. 2nd grade
3. K a.m. and 6th grade

P. 51

1. Tempa
2. Clinton
3. 5 inches
4. Clinton – 1 inch
5. 1986

P. 52

Check as a class activity.

Answer Key *(cont.)*

P. 53

Check as a class activity.

P. 54

1. 1;0, 2:2, 3:2, 4:4, 5:3, 6:5

2. week 6

3. week 1

4. last few weeks

P. 55

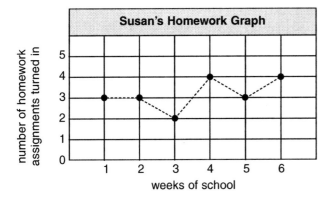

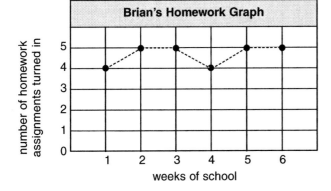

P. 56

The seventh week, Mr. Snuffles will probably weigh 35 pounds because he has gained 5 pounds a week.

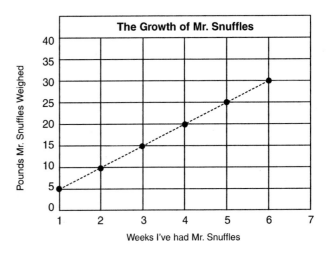

P. 57

Correct graph as a class activity.

1. a. 1 b. 8 c. 5 d. 4 e. 3 f. 7

2. weather-related answers; school-related answers

P. 58

Correct as a class activity. See if students can come to any conclusions about the prevalence of birds. (e.g., more bluejays than cardinals, etc.)

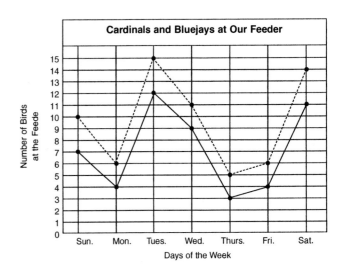

Answer Key *(cont.)*

P. 59

#1 = M, #2 = W, #3 = v

P. 60

1. leg

2. ears

3. ears, neck, back, knee, nostril, mouth, eye, forehead, shoulder

P. 61

1. True

2. False

3. True

4. True

5. True

P. 62

1. leaves

2. head

3. beard

4. kernel

5. stem

6. roots

P. 63

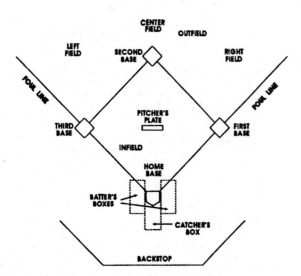

P. 66

Most answers will be:

1. orange, grapefruit, or lemon

2. pencil

3. honeycomb

4. nut

P. 67

1. 10:15 – 11:45

2. calendar, music, lunch

3. sharing, reading, writing, math, science, art, recess

P. 68

Check as a class activity. Encourage other ball sport ideas